The Cocktail Book

The Cocktail Book

A Sideboard Manual for Gentlemen

*" To know how to drink wine belongs
only to a cultivated taste ; to know how to
tempt guests to indulge in it with
pleasure belongs only to the host gifted
with rare tact and artistic discrimination."*

Publishers

JOHN HAMILTON, LTD.

LONDON

First printing - - November 1926
Second printing - December 1926

Printed in Great Britain

Introduction.

THIS book is not placed before the public as a " bar-tender's guide," nor is it a list of all the fancy combinations of various liquors invented to advertise certain establishments, or for imposing on the ignorant. It is a recipe book compiled for private use. By following the directions given, it is hoped that any gentleman will be able to provide his friends with most of the standard beverages, mixed in an acceptable manner.

FOR the use of those who have not been in the habit of handling wines, some hints are given concerning the care, the serving, and the combining of the various kinds, so that the qualities of a good dinner will not be marred by an injudicious disposition of the liquids.

Contents.

SOME RECENT FAVOURITES.

Miscellaneous Mixed Drinks.

Cocktails.

LET us have wine and women, mirth and laughter,
Sermons and soda-water the day after.

BYRON.

*T*HERE *are several ways of mixing a cocktail. Some prefer to shake it thoroughly ; by doing this it is made very cold. The best way to make a cocktail in a mixing glass is to stir it with a fork rather than with a spoon. By this method the ice is melted faster, cooling the liquor faster, and diluting it a little more.*

*I*T *is quite customary, in serving a dry cocktail, to put an olive, preferably stoned, in the glass. With a sweeter one a maraschino cherry, or a small preserved orange is generally given.*

The Real Tale of the Cock's Tail.

$\mathfrak{J}$N a famous old tavern not far from the Philipse Manor House, the site of what is now Yonkers on the Hudson, and the very centre of the most popular sport of the times, was blended the first delightful cocktail. If the descendants of William van Eyck, its jolly host, may be believed, no better place could be found along the length of the river, for William's stories were as good as the liquor that washed them down, and his liquors as honest and true and as sparkling withal as his daughter, Mistress Peggy, who gave them forth with such demure grace as made their serving doubly welcome to the thirsty gallants who thronged the bar and taproom.

NOW Master van Eyck loved but three

things well—his daughter, his cellar, and old Lightning, his great fighting bird, the acknowledged champion from New York to Albany. Indeed 'twere hard to tell which loved he the most, though his daughter was truly the idol of his heart.

(M)ISTRESS PEGGY'S lovers were many, and many were the strong potions quaffed, even when the driest throats were long since drowned in good liquor, because of her bewitching beauty,which gave added flavour and bouquet to the concoctions for which the bar was famous. But so well did she justify her father's confidence and her own good name that, though the gay bucks from town quarrelled and even fought for her favour, the most fortunate could not boast of the lightest thing to her discredit. On especial occasions she was wont to make for her father, and certain good friends of hers and old Lightning's, a most delicious beverage, the composition of which was secret, but which was so popular that it lacked naught but appropriate naming to give it more than local fame.

YOUNG Master Appleton, mate of the clipper-ship *Ranger*, had long been Mistress Peggy's ardent lover, and had even gone so far as to obtain mine host's reluctant consent that, when he could boast of a command, his daughter should be his an she would. Now Peggy, when she admitted to her coquettish self that she had a heart, knew that eventually she would be forced, in order to still its clamourings, to surrender it unconditionally into the keeping of a certain bold sailor ; but womanlike put off capitulating as long as she might. The time came, however, when the knowledge of his promotion gave Master Appleton the courage he had lacked to force the citadel which her coquetry had heretofore so jealously guarded ; and, when of a sudden Peggy's heart refused longer to be maligned by her mouth, and spake eloquently from out of bright eyes grown almost serious—before she could summon her mind to the fray—she was conquered, and, close embraced, was calling him dear whom, but the day before, she had flouted with reckless audacity.

EXCEPT when in training for a main, van Eyck's champion game-cock held his court in an apartment builded for him and adapted to his Majesty's special wants. None found favour in his master's eyes, nor forsooth in the eyes of Mistress Peggy, who failed in admiring and respectful homage to old Lightning. Worshipful attendance upon this pampered hero of many bloody victories, together with honest admiration for the daughter of his host, was looked upon as the surest way of gaining Master van Eyck's personal approval and the first step in advancing from favoured customer to friend.

IT was here that Peggy surrendered to her lover. And here it was that after a proper and reasonable time spent in the sweet dalliance due to such occasions, she mixed for him this most delightful of all drinks in order that he might face with proper spirit her bluff old father's temporary ire at the loss of his daughter. Just as the right proportions of bitters, root wine, and mellowest of old whiskey had been put to cook in a glass half-full of bits of purest ice, an interruption occurred, and the clarion voice of the brave old warrior bird was heard as if in celebration of the momentous event which had happened under his very eyes. As he plumed and shook himself after his effort, one of his royal tail feathers floated gently down towards his mistress

"LIGHTNING names the drink!" she cried, as she seized the feather and with it deftly stirred the glass's contents. And again, with a sweeping curtsey, holding the glass aloft:

"DRINK this *Cocktail*, sir, to your success with my father, and as a pledge to our future happiness!"

THUS was the drink named. And, in after days, when Master Appleton kept the tavern, its sign was the sign of the Cock's Tail, which ever proved an emblem of good fortune to him and his good wife, their children and their children's children.

C. F. P.

Cocktails.

Absinthe Cocktail.

Use Mixing Glass.

TWO dashes Angostura bitters ; two dashes gum syrup ; one pony absinthe. Fill with ice, mix well, and strain into a cocktail glass.

Algonquin Cocktail.

Use Mixing Glass.

FOUR dashes wormwood ; one portion Holland gin. Fill with ice, mix, and strain into a cocktail glass.

Apple Brandy Cocktail.

Use Mixing Glass.

TWO dashes Angostura bitters ; one portion apple brandy. Fill with ice, mix, and strain into a cocktail glass

7

Bamboo Cocktail.

Use Mixing Glass.

TWO dashes orange bitters ; one-half sherry and one-half Italian vermouth. Fill with ice, mix well, and strain into a cocktail glass

Blackthorn Cocktail.

Use Mixing Glass.

TWO dashes orange bitters ; two-thirds Sloe gin ; one-third Italian vermouth. Fill with ice, mix, and strain into a cocktail glass.

Brandy Cocktail.

Use Mixing Glass.

TWO dashes gum syrup ; two dashes Angostura bitters ; one portion brandy. Fill with ice, mix, and strain into a cocktail glass.

Brandy Cocktail—Fancy.

Use Mixing Glass.

THREE dashes maraschino ; two dashes bitters ; one dash orange bitters ; one portion brandy. Fill with ice, mix, and strain into a cocktail glass, the rim of which has been moistened with a piece of lemon and dipped in powdered sugar.

Brandy Cocktail—Old-fashioned.

CRUSH lump of sugar in a whiskey glass with sufficient hot water to cover the sugar. Add one lump of ice ; two dashes bitters ; a small piece lemon peel ; one portion brandy. Stir with small bar spoon. Serve, leaving spoon in glass.

Bronx Cocktail.

Use Mixing Glass.

TWO-THIRDS dry gin ; one-sixth Italian vermouth ; one-sixth French vermouth ; orange juice and orange pulp. Fill with ice, shake well, and strain into a cocktail glass.

Brut Cocktail.

THREE dashes orange bitters ; one portion Italian vermouth ; three dashes acid phosphate. Fill with ice, shake well, and strain into a cocktail glass

Calisaya Cocktail.

Use Mixing Glass.

TWO dashes orange bitters ; one-third sherry wine ; two-thirds Calisaya. Fill with ice, stir well, and strain into a cocktail glass.

Champagne Cocktail.

Use Long, Thin Glass.

ONE lump cut loaf sugar, saturated with Angostura bitters ; one lump ice ; one piece lemon peel. Fill glass with cold champagne, stir with spoon, and serve.

Champagne Cocktail Fancy.

AS above, adding one slice each of orange and pineapple.

Cholera Cocktail.

Use Bar Glass.

HALF a teaspoonful Jamaica ginger;
half a pony brandy; half a pony
port wine; one and a half ponies cherry
brandy, one and a half ponies blackberry
brandy. Grate nutmeg, and stir in with
spoon. Use no ice.

Chocolate Cocktail.

Use Mixing Glass.

ONE fresh egg; one dash bitters; one
portion port wine; one teaspoonful
fine sugar. Fill with ice, shake well, and
strain into a cocktail glass.

Cider Cocktail.

Use Thin Cider Glass.

ONE lump cut loaf sugar, saturated with
bitters; one lump ice; one small
piece lemon peel Fill with cold cider,
stir with spoon, and serve.

Clover Club Cocktail.

Use Mixing Glass.

ONE portion dry gin ; juice of one-half lime ; white of one egg ; tablespoonful Grenadine or strawberry syrup. Fill with ice, shake well, strain into a large cocktail glass, and serve with sprig of mint on top.

Coffee Cocktail.

Use Mixing Glass.

ONE teaspoonful powdered sugar ; one fresh egg ; one portion port wine; one portion brandy. Fill with ice, shake thoroughly, and strain into a large cocktail glass. Grate a little nutmeg on top before serving.

Cooperstown Cocktail.

Use Mixing Glass.

JUICE of quarter orange ; one-third Italian vermouth ; two-thirds dry gin ; sprig of mint. Fill with ice, shake well, and strain into a cocktail glass.

Country Cocktail.

Use Mixing Glass.

TWO dashes orange bitters ; two dashes Angostura bitters ; one piece lemon peel ; one portion rye whiskey. Fill with ice, mix well, and strain into a cocktail glass.

Deronda Cocktail.

Use Mixing Glass.

ONE-THIRD Calisaya ; two-thirds Plymouth gin. Fill with ice, mix well, and strain into a cocktail glass.

Dubonnet Cocktail.

Use Mixing Glass.

ONE-THIRD dry gin ; two-thirds Dubonnet. Fill with ice, stir well (do not shake), and strain into a cocktail glass.

Duchess Cocktail.

Use Mixing Glass.

ONE-THIRD French vermouth ; one-third Italian vermouth ; one-third absinthe. Fill with ice, shake well, and strain into a cocktail glass.

Duplex Cocktail.

Use Mixing Glass.

THREE dashes orange bitters ; one-half Italian vermouth ; one-half French vermouth ; three dashes acid phosphate. Fill with ice, shake well, and strain into a cocktail glass.

Florida Cocktail.

Use Medium-sized Tumbler.

FILL glass three-quarters with ice, juice of one lemon and one and a half orange. Stir with spoon and serve.

Gaby Cocktail.

Use Mixing Glass.

ONE-THIRD dry gin ; one-third crème d'Yvette ; one-third crème de menthe (white). Fill with ice, shake well, and strain into a cocktail glass.

Gin Cocktail.

Use Mixing Glass.

TWO dashes bitters ; two dashes gum syrup ; one portion Holland gin. Fill with ice, mix, and strain into a cocktail glass.

Gin Cocktail—Old Fashioned.

PUT a lump of sugar in a whiskey glass, and cover it with hot water. Crush the sugar ; add lump of ice, two dashes bitters, small piece lemon peel, one portion Holland gin. Mix with small bar spoon, and serve with spoon in glass

Gin Cocktail—Old-fashioned Tom.

MAKE the same as an Old-fashioned Holland Gin Cocktail, using Tom in the place of Holland gin.

Harvard Cocktail.

Use Mixing Glass.

ONE dash gum syrup; three dashes Angostura bitters; one-half Italian vermouth; one-half brandy. Fill with ice, mix and strain into a cocktail glass, then fill with seltzer and serve quickly.

H. P. W. Cocktail.

Use Mixing Glass.

ONE-SIXTH Italian vermouth; one-sixth French vermouth; two-thirds dry gin. Fill with ice, shake well, and strain into a whiskey tumbler. Twist of orange peel dropped into tumbler.

Irish Cocktail.

Use Mixing Glass.

ONE dash orange bitters ; one-third French vermouth ; two-thirds crême de menthe (green). Fill with ice, shake well, and strain into a cocktail glass.

Jack Rose Cocktail.

Use Mixing Glass.

ONE-QUARTER dry gin ; three-quarters apple brandy ; juice of half lime ; tablespoonful of Grenadine syrup. Fill with ice, shake well, and strain into a large cocktail glass.

Jamaica Rum Cocktail.

Use Mixing Glass.

TWO dashes gum syrup ; two dashes orange bitters ; two dashes bitters ; one portion Jamaica rum. Fill with ice, mix, and strain into a cocktail glass.

Jersey Cocktail.

Use Thin Cider Glass.

ONE lump ice ; one-half teaspoonful fine sugar ; two dashes bitters ; one piece lemon peel. Fill up with cold cider. Stir well, and serve while effervescent

Kemble House Cocktail.

Use Mixing Glass.

FOUR dashes Fernet-Branca bitters; one-quarter French vermouth ; three-quarters orange gin. Fill with ice, shake well, and strain into a cocktail glass.

Lemon Cocktail.

Use Mixing Glass.

TWO dashes Angostura bitters ; two dashes gum syrup ; lemon juice   Fill with ice, mix, and strain into a cocktail glass.

Liberal Cocktail.

Use Mixing Glass.

ONE dash syrup ; half Picon bitters ; one-half whiskey. Fill with ice, mix, strain into a cocktail glass, and put a small piece of lemon peel on top.

Lone Tree Cocktail.

ONE-HALF Italian vermouth ; one-half Tom gin. No bitters. Fill with ice, mix, and strain into a cocktail glass.

Manhattan Cocktail.

Use Mixing Glass.

TWO dashes gum syrup ; two dashes Angostura bitters ; one-half Italian vermouth ; one-half whiskey. Fill with ice, mix, and strain. Add a small twist of lemon peel.

Manhattan Cocktail —Dry.

MAKE the same as a Manhattan cocktail, leaving out the syrup.

Manhattan Cocktail — Extra Dry.

MAKE the same as the dry cocktail, using French vermouth instead of Italian.

Marguerite Cocktail.

Use Mixing Glass.

TWO-THIRDS Plymouth gin ; one-third French vermouth. Fill with ice, shake well, and strain into a cocktail glass.

Martini Cocktail.

Use Mixing Glass.

THREE dashes orange bitters; two-thirds Tom gin; one-third Italian vermouth; small piece lemon peel. Fill with ice, mix, and strain into a cocktail glass.

Martini Cocktail — Dry.

Use Mixing Glass.

TWO dashes orange bitters; two-thirds dry gin; one-third French vermouth; small piece lemon peel Fill with ice, mix, and strain into a cocktail glass.

Medford Rum Cocktail.

Use Mixing Glass.

ONE dash gum syrup; two dashes bitters; one portion Medford rum. Fill with ice, mix, and strain into a cocktail glass.

Metropole Cocktail.

TWO dashes gum syrup ; two dashes Peychaud bitters ; one dash orange bitters ; one-half brandy ; one-half French vermouth. Fill with ice, mix, and strain into a cocktail glass.

Narragansett Cocktail.

TWO-THIRDS whiskey ; one-third Italian vermouth ; one dash absinthe. No bitters. Fill with ice, mix, and strain into a cocktail glass

Navy Cocktail.

JUICE of quarter orange ; one dash Angostura bitters ; one-quarter Italian vermouth ; three-quarters Bacardi rum. Fill with ice, shake well, and strain into a cocktail glass.

New Orleans Cocktail.

Use Mixing Glass.

ONE dash Angostura bitters ; one portion Italian vermouth. Fill with ice, shake well, strain into a star champagne glass. Fill with soda water.

Orange Blossom Cocktail.

Use Mixing Glass.

JUICE of quarter orange ; one portion dry gin. Fill with ice, shake well, and strain into a cocktail glass.

Oyster Cocktail.

Use Tumbler.

A FEW dashes lemon juice ; one dash Tobasco sauce ; one teaspoonful vinegar ; a few dashes tomato catsup ; six oysters with all their liquor. Season to taste with pepper and salt. Mix, and serve with small fork in the glass.

Perfect Cocktail.

Use Mixing Glass.

ONE-THIRD French vermouth ; one-third Italian vermouth ; one-third dry gin. Fill with ice, mix, and strain into a cocktail glass.

Princeton Cocktail.

Use Mixing Glass.

THREE dashes orange bitters ; three-quarters Tom gin. Fill with ice, mix, and strain into a cocktail glass. Add one-quarter port wine carefully, and let it settle to bottom before serving.

Puritan Cocktail.

Use Mixing Glass.

THREE dashes orange bitters ; one spoonful yellow chartreuse ; two-thirds Plymouth gin ; one-third French vermouth. Fill with ice, mix, and strain into a cocktail glass.

Queen's Cocktail.

Use Mixing Glass.

TABLESPOONFUL of grape fruit juice ; one-third Italian vermouth ; two-thirds dry gin. Fill with ice, shake well, and strain into a cocktail glass.

Riding Club Cocktail.

Use Mixing Glass.

ONE glass Angostura bitters ; small spoonful Horsford's acid phosphate ; one portion Calisaya. Fill with ice, mix, and strain into a cocktail glass.

Rob Roy Cocktail.

Use Mixing Glass.

TWO dashes orange bitters ; two-thirds Scotch whiskey ; one-third Italian vermouth. Fill with ice, mix, and strain into a cocktail glass. Serve an olive in the glass.

Sazarac Cocktail.

Use Whiskey Tumbler.

FOUR dashes absinthe, turn glass around slowly ; one lump sugar ; three dashes Peychaud bitters ; one portion whiskey ; one cube ice ; sprig of mint. Stir and serve in tumbler.

Soda Cocktail.

Use Large Glass.

THREE or four lumps of ice ; one tea-spoonful fine sugar ; three dashes Angostura bitters ; one bottle plain soda, or lemon soda ; one twist lemon peel. Stir well and serve while effervescent.

Star Cocktail.

Use Mixing Glass.

TWO dashes gum syrup ; three dashes orange bitters ; one-half apple brandy ; one-half Italian vermouth. Fill with ice, mix, strain into a cocktail glass, and add small twist of lemon peel.

Thorndike Cocktail.

Use Mixing Glass.

JUICE of quarter orange ; one-third Italian vermouth ; two-thirds dry gin Fill with ice, shake well, and strain into a cocktail glass.

26

Trilby Cocktail.

Use Mixing Glass.

THREE dashes orange bitters ; three dashes acid phosphate ; two-thirds whiskey ; one-third Calisaya. Fill with ice, mix, and strain into a cocktail glass.

Turf Cocktail.

Use Mixing Glass.

TWO dashes bitters ; one-third Italian vermouth ; two-thirds Medford rum Fill glass with ice, stir well, and strain into a cocktail glass

Tuxedo Cocktail.

Use Mixing Glass.

ONE dash Angostura bitters ; one spoonful sherry ; one-half Tom gin ; one-half Italian vermouth. Fill with ice, mix, and strain into a cocktail glass

Vermouth Cocktail.

Use Mixing Glass.

TWO dashes Boker's or Peychaud bitters; one portion Italian vermouth. Fill with ice, mix, and strain into a cocktail glass.

Vermouth Cocktail Dry.

MAKE the same as Vermouth Cocktail, substituting French vermouth for Italian.

Vermouth Cocktail Fancy.

Use Mixing Glass.

THREE dashes maraschino, two dashes bitters; one portion Italian vermouth; one dash orange bitters. Fill with ice, mix, and strain into a cocktail glass, the rim of which has been moistened with a piece of lemon peel and dipped into powdered sugar.

Vermouth Cocktail - French.

Use Mixing Glass.

THREE dashes orange bitters ; one portion French vermouth. Fill with ice, mix, and strain into a cocktail glass.

Whiskey Cocktail.

Use Mixing Glass.

TWO dashes gum syrup ; two dashes Angostura bitters ; one portion rye whiskey. Fill with ice, mix, and strain into a cocktail glass. Add a twist of lemon peel.

Whiskey Cocktail --Fancy.

Use Mixing Glass.

TWO dashes maraschino ; two dashes Angostura bitters ; one dash orange bitters ; one portion rye whiskey. Fill with ice and mix till very cold. Strain into a cocktail glass, the rim of which has been moistened with lemon juice and dipped into powdered sugar.

Whiskey Cocktail —Old-fashioned.

PUT a lump of sugar in a whiskey glass ; add enough hot water to cover the sugar. Crush the sugar ; add a lump of ice, two dashes bitters, one portion whiskey, small piece lemon peel. Mix with small spoon, and serve with spoon in glass.

Yale Cocktail.

Use Mixing Glass.

THREE dashes orange bitters ; one dash bitters ; piece lemon peel ; one portion Tom gin. Fill with ice, mix, and strain into a cocktail glass ; add a squirt of siphon seltzer

Some Recent Favourites

Bacardi Rum Cocktail.

Use Shaker.

ONE teaspoon sugar; one portion Bacardi rum; half portion orange juice; half portion lemon juice. Fill with ice, shake until very cold, and strain into a cocktail glass

Bacardi Rum Cocktail—Dry.

Use Shaker.

ONE dash grenadine; one portion Bacardi rum; one portion lemon juice Fill with ice, shake until very cold, and strain into a cocktail glass.

Daiquiri Cocktail.

Use Shaker.

ONE portion grenadine syrup, three portions Bacardi rum, juice of one lime. Shake well, and strain into a cocktail glass.

31

Ladies' Delight Cocktail.

Use Shaker.

ONE dash of lemon juice ; one dash of Curacao ; half teaspoon powdered sugar ; one portion gin ; one portion orange juice. Fill with ice, shake well, and strain into a cocktail glass.

Ma Cherie Cocktail.

Use Shaker.

ONE dash lemon juice ; two good-sized sprays fresh mint ; one portion sherry. Fill with ice, shake until very cold, and strain into a cocktail glass.

Mint Spray Cocktail.

Use Shaker.

ONE dash of lemon juice ; half teaspoon powdered sugar ; one good-sized spray fresh mint ; one portion gin ; one portion orange juice. Fill with ice, shake very thoroughly, and strain into a cocktail glass.

Nutley Special Cocktail.

Use Shaker.

ONE portion dry gin; one-quarter portion prepared orange juice; small amount Five Fruit syrup; a few sprigs of fresh mint. Fill with ice, shake well, and strain into a cocktail glass.

Orange Blossom Special Cocktail.

Use Shaker.

ONE portion gin; one portion orange juice. Dip a spoon into honey, and dissolve in the gin only what honey adheres to the spoon. Then add the orange juice, fill with ice, shake well, and strain into a cocktail glass.

Page Court Cocktail.

Use Shaker.

ONE portion rye whiskey*; half portion Jamaica Rum; half portion dry gin; juice of one orange; dash of bitters. Fill with ice, shake well, and strain into a cocktail glass.

* Scotch whiskey can be substituted, and the bitters omitted.

Pearl Cocktail.

Use Shaker.

ONE portion French Vermouth, two portions dry gin ; two or three dashes of Orange Bitters ; three or four dashes of Onion Juice. Shake well, and serve in fancy cocktail glass with small pearl onion in place of the usual olive.

Pineapple Blossom Cocktail.

Use Shaker.

ONE portion Scotch or rye whiskey ; half portion pineapple juice : half portion lemon juice. Fill with ice, shake well, and strain into a cocktail glass

Pink Beauty Cocktail.

Use Shaker.

ONE dash of Five Fruit syrup ; one portion gin ; half portion Vermouth. Fill with ice, shake well, and strain into a cocktail glass.

Rosy Cocktail.

Use Shaker.

ONE portion gin ; half portion claret ; half portion orange juice. Fill with ice, shake well, and strain into a cocktail glass.

Standard Cocktail

Use Shaker.

ONE portion gin ; half portion French Vermouth ; half portion Italian Vermouth ; three-fourths portion orange juice. Fill with ice, shake well, and strain into a cocktail glass.

Stirrup Cup Cocktail.

Use Shaker.

ONE portion Scotch or Rye whiskey ; one portion orange juice. Fill with ice, shake thoroughly and strain into a cocktail glass.

Sweet Cider Cocktail.

Use Shaker.

TEASPOON grenadine syrup ; one portion gin ; one portion sweet cider. Fill with ice, shake well, and strain into a cocktail glass.

T.N.T. Cocktail.

Use Shaker.

HALF teaspoon powdered sugar ; one raw egg ; one portion brandy ; one portion port. Fill with ice, shake very thoroughly, and strain into a glass.

Zelli's Special Cocktail.

Use Shaker.

TWO portions gin ; one portion dry Vermouth ; two limes cut into small pieces and added, peels and all, to the shaker ; dash of grenadine. Fill with ice, shake well, and strain into a cocktail glass.

Miscellaneous Mixed Drinks.

THEY that love mirth, let them heartily drink,
'Tis the only receipt to make sorrow sink.

JONSON.

Miscellaneous Mixed Drinks.

Absinthe Frappe.

Use Mixing Glass.

ONE pony absinthe. Fill glass with fine ice, shake well, and strain into a cocktail glass.

Blue Blazes.

Use Two Hot-water Glasses.

ONE lump sugar ; one portion Scotch whiskey. Fill glass with hot water, ignite and pour from one glass to another. Add a little grated nutmeg.

Brandy Flip.

Use Mixing Glass.

ONE teaspoonful sugar ; one wine glass brandy ; one fresh egg Fill glass half full of fine shaved ice. Shake well in shaker Strain into star champagne glass, and grate a little nutmeg on top.

Brandy Smash.

Use Small Tumbler.

THREE or four sprigs of fresh mint; cover bottom with water; one lump sugar; crush the mint; add one or two lumps of ice; one portion brandy. Stir well, and serve in same glass.

Buttered Rum.

Use Tumbler.

ONE lump sugar; dissolve in hot water; one-third rum; two-thirds hot water; butter the size of a walnut. Grate a little nutmeg on top.

Café au Kirsch.*

Use Mixing Glass.

FILL glass half-full of fine ice; half a cup of hot black coffee; one pony Kirschwasser. Shake, and strain into a cocktail glass.

* After-dinner drink.

California Absinthe.

Use Mixing Glass.

ONE pony absinthe. Fill glass with fine ice. Shake well, strain into star champagne glass, and fill with siphon.

Champagne Cobbler.

Use Delicate Wine Glass.

SMALL lump sugar. Fill glass with shaved ice. Pour in champagne till the glass is full. Serve with straw, and decorate with fruit and leaves.

Champagne Cup.

Use Glass Pitcher.

HALF tablespoonful sugar ; one rind of lemon ; three slices orange ; three slices lemon ; berries ; one slice cucumber peel ; one pony brandy ; one pony maraschino ; one pony white curaçao ; one wine glass sherry ; one quart champagne ; one bottle soda ; two or three large lumps of ice. Ornament with fresh mint.

Cider Cup.

SAME as Champagne Cup, using cider in the place of champagne

Circus Rickey.

Use Medium-sized Tumbler.

JUICE one lime ; leave half of the pressed lime in glass ; one lump ice ; one portion dry gin ; tablespoon Grenadine syrup. Fill with siphon

Claret Cobbler.

Use Large Glass.

ONE tablespoonful powdered sugar. Fill glass with shaved ice. Pour full of claret. Shake in shaker. Ornament with fruit and serve with straws.

Claret Cup.

SAME as Champagne Cup, using claret in the place of champagne

Claret Punch.

Use Large Glass.

ONE tablespoonful powdered sugar ; two dashes lemon juice Fill glass with shaved ice. Fill with claret. Shake well. Ornament with fruit, serve with straws.

Egg Nog.

Use Mixing Glass.

THREE-QUARTERS tablespoon sugar ; one wine glass whiskey or brandy ; one-half glass shaved ice ; one fresh egg. Fill glass with fresh milk Shake well, strain into a large glass, and grate over it a little nutmeg.

43

Bowl of Egg Nog.

This recipe is for making a two-gallon bowl full.

TWO pounds fine powdered sugar; twenty fresh eggs. Have the yolks separated and beaten till thin as water. Add the yolks to the sugar, and dissolve well with spoon. Two quarts good old brandy; one and half pints St. Croix or Jamaica rum; one and a half gallons rich milk. Mix the ingredients well with ladle, stirring continually while pouring in the milk. Beat the whites of eggs to stiff froth. Pour this froth carefully over the mixture. In serving, dip out with ladle. Put a little of the white on the top of each help, and grate on a little nutmeg. Serve in punch glasses.

Fog Horn.

Use Large Tumbler.

ONE portion dry gin ; juice of half lime, one lump ice. Fill with ginger ale.

Gin Daisy.

Use Mixing Glass.

ONE teaspoonful fine sugar ; juice of half lime ; one portion Tom gin ; tablespoonful raspberry syrup ; fill with ice. Shake well ; strain into tumbler ; fill up with siphon ; ornament with fruit and serve.

Gin Fizz.

Use Mixing Glass.

ONE-HALF tablespoonful sugar ; three or four dashes lemon juice ; one wine glass Tom gin. Fill glass with ice ; shake ; strain into fizz glass, and fill up with soda.

Gin Rickey.

JUICE one lime ; leave half of the pressed lime in glass ; one lump ice ; one wine glass Tom gin.   Fill with siphon

Golden Fizz.

Use Mixing Glass.

ONE-HALF tablespoonful sugar ; three or four dashes lemon juice ; one wine glass Tom gin ; yolk of one egg   Fill glass with ice, shake well, and strain into fizz glass.   Fill with siphon

Hot Applejack.

Use Hot Water Glass.

TWO lumps sugar. Fill glass two-thirds full of boiling water and dissolve sugar. One wine glass applejack ; one slice lemon   Serve with spoon.

Hot Apple Toddy.

Use Hot Water Glass.

HALF tablespoonful sugar. Fill glass two-thirds with boiling water. One wine glass applejack ; two spoonfuls baked apple Grate over a little nutmeg, and serve with spoon.

Hot Irish.

TWO lumps sugar. Fill glass two-thirds with boiling water ; dissolve sugar. One wine glass full Irish whiskey ; one slice lemon peel. Serve with spoon.

Hot Scotch.

Use Hot Water Glass.

TWO lumps sugar. Fill glass two-thirds full boiling water, and dissolve sugar One wine glass Scotch whiskey ; one slice lemon peel. Serve with spoon

Hot Spiced Rum.

Use Hot Water Glass.

ONE or two lumps loaf sugar. Fill glass two-thirds full boiling water, and dissolve sugar ; one wine glass Jamaica rum ; six or eight cloves Serve with spoon. Good for sore throat.

John Collins.

Use Long Glass.

ONE-HALF teaspoonful sugar ; five or six dashes lemon juice ; one wine glass Holland gin. Dissolve the sugar with spoon ; add three or four lumps of ice, and pour in a bottle of soda water.

Maiden's Dream.*

Use Pousse Café Glass.

THREE-QUARTERS pony Benedictine, fill with cream, and serve.

* After-dinner drink.

Mamie Taylor.

Use Large Glass.

JUICE of half lime ; one portion Scotch whiskey ; one bottle ginger ale ; one lump ice. Stir well and serve.

Medford Rum Punch.

Use Large Glass.

THREE-QUARTERS tablespoonful powdered sugar ; two or three dashes lemon juice. Dissolve with a little water. Fill glass with fine shaved ice. One and a quarter wine glass Medford rum. Shake well, and ornament with fruit Serve with straws.

Milk Punch.

Use Mixing Glass.

THREE-QUARTERS tablespoonful sugar ; one wine glass whiskey or brandy ; one-half glass shaved ice. Fill glass with good milk, shake, and strain into large glass Grate a little nutmeg on top.

Mint Julep.

Use Large Glass.

ONE-HALF tablespoonful sugar ; one-half wine glass water ; three or four sprigs fresh mint. Fill up glass with shaved ice. Do not stir or shake, but let stand three or four minutes till glass is frosted. One wine glass Bourbon whiskey Ornament with cluster of mint.

Mint Julep—Brandy.

MAKE the same as above, using brandy instead of Bourbon whiskey.

Morning-Glory Fizz.

Use Mixing Glass.

ONE tablespoonful fine sugar ; juice of half lemon ; one portion Scotch whiskey ; three dashes absinthe ; white of one egg. Fill glass with ice, shake well, strain into fizz glass, and fill with siphon

New York Sour.

Use Mixing Glass.

ONE teaspoonful fine sugar ; juice of half lemon, one portion rye whiskey. Fill with ice, stir well, strain into sour glass, float a little claret on top, and serve.

Peach Blow Fizz.

Use Mixing Glass.

ONE tablespoonful sugar ; juice of half-lemon ; one portion Tom gin ; tablespoonful Grenadine syrup ; three dashes cream. Fill with ice, shake well, strain into fizz glass and fill with siphon

Pick Me Up.

Use Mixing Glass.

ONE-QUARTER Fernet-Branca bitters ; one-quarter Italian vermouth ; one-half rye whiskey. Fill with ice, shake well, and strain into a cocktail glass.

Picon High Ball.

ONE portion Amer-Picon ; two dashes Grenadine syrup ; one twist orange peel ; one lump ice. Fill with siphon and serve.

Pigeon Wing.*

PLACE cherry in bottom of glass ; one-third maraschino ; one-third crême d'Yvette ; one-third cream. Pour each slowly, so that the three ingredients do not run together.

* After-dinner drink.

Planters' Punch.

ONE portion juice of fresh limes ; two portions sugar ; three portions water ; four portions Old Jamaica rum. Fill glass with shaved ice, shake well, add dash red pepper if desired, and serve with straw

Port and Starboard.

Use Pousse Café Glass.

ONE-HALF orange curaçao ; one-half green mint. Pour carefully so that they will not mix.

Port Wine Flip.

Use Mixing Glass.

ONE teaspoonful powdered sugar ; one wine glass port wine ; one fresh egg. Fill glass half-full of shaved ice. Shake well, strain into star champagne glass, and grate a little nutmeg on top.

Port Wine Sangaree.

Use Mixing Glass.

ONE teaspoonful sugar dissolved in a little water ; one wine glass port wine ; five or six lumps of ice. Stir with spoon. Strain into a star champagne glass, and grate a little nutmeg on top.

Pousse Cafe.*

Use Pousse Café Glass.

ONE-SIXTH each of the following : Raspberry syrup, maraschino, orange curaçao, yellow Chartreuse, green Chartreuse, and brandy. Pour in carefully so that they will not mix.

* After-dinner drink.

Pousse L'Amour.*

Use Sherry Glass.

ONE-QUARTER sherry glass maraschino ; yolk of egg, cold ; quarter of a glass of vanilla ; quarter of a glass of cognac Take great care that the egg does not mix with the cordials.

* After-dinner drink.

Ramos Fizz.

Use Mixing Glass.

ONE tablespoonful sugar ; juice of half lemon ; white of one egg ; one portion Tom gin ; three dashes orange flower water. Fill with ice, shake well, strain into fizz glass and fill with siphon.

Remsen Cooler.

Use Large Glass.

ONE whole rind of lemon ; three lumps of ice ; one portion Tom gin ; one bottle plain soda.

Rhine Wine Cobbler.

ONE tablespoonful powdered sugar ; one-half glass water. Dissolve well with spoon. Fill glass with shaved ice. Fill with Rhine wine. Shake well and ornament with fruits. Serve with straws

Rickety Scotch.

Use Medium-sized Tumbler.

HALF a lime squeezed into glass ; two dashes lemon juice ; one wine glass Scotch whiskey ; one lump ice. Fill with siphon.

Royal Fizz.

Use Mixing Glass.

ONE tablespoonful fine sugar ; three or four dashes lemon juice ; one wine glass Tom gin ; one egg. Fill glass with ice, shake well, strain into fizz glass, and fill with siphon.

Royal Plush.

Use Glass Pitcher.

TWO or three large lumps ice ; one pint champagne ; one pint of Burgundy. Pour into glass pitcher and stir with spoon.

Sam Ward.*

RIND of one lemon placed in cocktail glass ; fill with fine ice ; then fill the glass with one-half yellow Chartreuse and one-half orange curaçao.

* After-dinner drink.

Sauterne Cobbler.

Use Large Glass.

THREE-QUARTERS tablespoonful powdered sugar; one-quarter wine glass water Dissolve well with spoon Fill glass with fine shaved ice; one and a half wine glassfuls sauterne Shake well and ornament with fruit Serve with straws.

Sauterne or Hock Cup.

Use Glass Pitcher.

ONE tablespoonful sugar; rind of one lemon; three slices orange; three slices lemon; berries; one slice cucumber peel; one pony brandy; one pony maraschino; one wine glass sherry; one quart sauterne or hock; one bottle soda; two or three lumps ice. Ornament with fresh mint.

Shandy Gaff.

HALF beer or ale ; half ginger ale. This is best if the parts are poured in together.

Sherry Cobbler.

Use Large Glass.

ONE tablespoonful powdered sugar dissolved in a little water. Fill glass with shaved ice. Fill with sherry ; shake well. Ornament with fruits and serve with straws.

Sherry Flip.

Use Mixing Glass.

ONE teaspoonful powdered sugar ; one wine glass sherry wine ; one fresh egg. Fill glass half-full shaved ice. Shake well; strain into star champagne glass and grate a little nutmeg on top

Silver Fizz.

Use Mixing Glass.

ONE tablespoonful sugar ; three or four dashes lemon juice ; one wine glass Tom gin ; white of one egg. Fill glass with ice, shake well, strain into fizz glass, and fill with siphon.

Souisesse.

Use Large Glass.

ONE pony absinthe ; white of one egg ; two dashes Anisette. Fill with shaved ice Shake very well, and fill with siphon.

St. Croix Rum Sour.

Use Mixing Glass.

HALF tablespoonful sugar ; two or three dashes lemon juice ; one squirt of seltzer Dissolve well. One wine glass St. Croix rum. Fill glass with ice, stir well, and strain into sour glass. Ornament with fruit.

Stinger.*

Use Mixing Glass.

ONE-THIRD white crême de menthe ; two-thirds brandy. Fill with ice, shake well, and strain into a cocktail glass.

* After-dinner drink.

Syracuse Cooler.

Use Large Glass.

RIND of whole lemon, three lumps ice, one portion Medford rum ; one bottle ginger ale.

Three Trees.*

Use Pousse Café Glass.

ONE-THIRD each, green, white and ruby crême de menthe Pour slowly so that they will not mix.

* After-dinner drink.

Tom Collins.

Use Large Glass.

MAKE same as John Collins, using Tom gin instead of Holland.

Tom and Jerry.

Use a Mug.

ONE egg. Beat the white and yoke separately, then beat together, with one tablespoonful sugar, one-quarter portion rum, three-quarters portion brandy. Add hot milk and serve with nutmeg on top.

Velvet.

Use Large Pitcher.

ONE bottle of stout; one bottle of champagne. Stir well and serve.

Ward Eight.

Use Goblet.

ONE teaspoonful fine sugar ; juice of half lemon ; one tablespoonful Grenadine syrup ; one portion rye whiskey ; one lump ice. Fill glass with siphon, stir well, ornament with fruit, and serve

Whiskey Rickey.

SAME as gin rickey, using whiskey in the place of gin.

Whiskey Sour.

SAME as St. Croix Rum Sour, using whiskey in place of rum.

Some Recent Favourites.

Bandol Melange.

ONE portion Kümmel; one portion Jamaica rum. Pour into a champagne glass full of shaved ice. Allow to set for one hour. Serve with a straw.

Shelbourne Cooler

Use Shaker.

WHITE of one egg; one portion Gordon gin; juice of one orange; one-quarter portion of Grenadine. Fill with ice, shake well, and strain into a tall glass, and then fill with soda water.

Non=Alcoholic Drinks.

> *THE cups*
> *That cheer but not inebriate.*
>
> Cowper.

Non=Alcoholic Drinks.

Boston Cooler.

Use Large Glass.

RIND of one lemon ; three lumps ice ; bottle sarsaparilla; bottle ginger ale.

Brunswick.

Use Mixing Glass.

HALF tablespoonful sugar ; one fresh egg ; half glass shaved ice. Fill glass with ice, shake, strain into large glass, and grate nutmeg on top. Serve with straws.

Bull's Eye.

RIND of one lemon ; three lumps ice ; half pint cider ; one bottle ginger ale.

Horse's Neck.

RIND one lemon ; two or three lumps ice ; one bottle ginger ale. Stir with spoon.

Lemonade.

TABLESPOONFUL sugar ; three or four dashes lemon juice ; three or four lumps of ice. Fill glass with water, shake well, and ornament with fruits. Serve with straws.

Egg Lemonade.

Use Mixing Glass.

ONE fresh egg ; tablespoonful sugar ; four or five dashes lemon juice ; four or five lumps of ice. Fill with water, shake well, and strain into a large glass.

Soda Lemonade.

Use Large Glass.

TABLESPOONFUL sugar ; three or four dashes lemon juice ; three or four lumps ice ; bottle plain soda. Stir well with spoon, remove ice and serve.

Limeade.

Use Large Glass.

TABLESPOONFUL sugar ; juice three limes. Fill glass half-full shaved ice. Fill with water, shake well, and dress with fruit. Serve with straws.

Mule's Collar.

Use Large Glass.

JUICE one lime ; one dash Angostura bitters ; three lumps ice ; one bottle dry ginger ale.

Orangeade.

Use Large Glass.

TABLESPOONFUL sugar Squeeze the juice of one orange. Fill glass half-full with fine shaved ice. Fill with water, shake well, and dress with fruit. Serve with straws.

Care and Serving of Wines.

GIVE me a bowl of wine—
In this I bury all unkindness.
SHAKESPEARE.

Care and Serving of Wines.

WINE does not differ from any other luxury in this world. Each person has his own ideas and tastes concerning it. On this account, no hard and fast rules can be laid down. There are, however, certain customs which have been almost universally adopted by " good livers." These will be embodied in the following few lines.

AS relating to beer or wine in the cask, it is not necessary to give any instructions. Beer served from the keg is an article scarcely ever seen in the household. If one has wine in the barrel, he must have a professional to bottle it, who is an expert at the business.

BEER or ale should not be served too cold. It may be placed near the ice, with the bottle in an upright position. It should not come in contact with the ice, as it would be chilled. In pouring it, care should be taken not to shake the bottle, so as to stir up the sediment.

CLARET, Burgundy, Sauterne, hock, port, sherry, and other light wines, should always be kept with the bottle in a horizontal position. They should be served at a temperature of 60°-70°, great care being taken not to disturb the dregs.

CHAMPAGNE should always be kept on its side It should be served as cold as is possible. When it is put on the ice care should be taken not to soak off the labels, and no more should be cooled than is to be used, as it detracts from its vitality to chill and then warm it If one has to cool champagne in a hurry, it can be well done by turning the bottle in an ice-cream freezer packed with ice and salt.

CORDIALS can be kept at any moderate temperature, and, like any other sweet substances, they should be protected from the invasion of insects

LIQUORS, such as rum, whiskey, brandy, and gin, are generally bought in bulk, and need very little care. They are generally kept in a decanter, and served directly from the same ; if any particular temperature is desired, it is regulated by the addition of hot or cold water. If liquor is to be kept a great number of years it should be bottled, the bottles laid in a horizontal position, and recorked from time to time.

Choice of Wines for Dinner.

DRINK no longer water, but use a little wine for thy stomach's sake.

1 TIMOTHY v. 23.

Choice of Wines for Dinner.

THE variety of wines to be served with a dinner depends largely on the rest of the menu.

BEFORE a stag dinner of any kind, it is generally customary to serve either a cocktail, or a glass of sherry with a dash of bitters in it. When ladies are present this is generally dispensed with.

FOR a small dinner of four or five courses, it is generally good form to serve sherry with the soup and fish, followed by a Sauterne, Hock, or Rhine wine, and nothing further.

AT very elaborate feasts the number of wines introduced is almost unlimited ; but the following list is believed to contain the essential features :

WITH soup, sherry ; with fish, white wine ; with meats, Burgundy and Roman or kirsch punch ; with roast meats or poultry, champagne ; with entrées, champagne ; with game and salads, champagne, or particularly rich claret or Burgundy ; with dessert and coffee, a little burnt brandy is the most correct liquor, although any kind of cordial is largely served. The chief principle to be followed is that the choicer and heavier wines should follow the lighter ones.

THE END

BRISTOL : BURLEIGH LTD., AT THE BURLEIGH PRESS

www.ingramcontent.com/pod-product-compliance
Lightning Source LLC
Chambersburg PA
CBHW071906020426
42331CB00010B/2691